My Life with
Lupus
and Other Annoying Things

*A Personal Story Of Struggle,
Triumph and Faith*

Linda Joy Fullerton Swift

ISBN 978-1-0980-4428-2 (paperback)
ISBN 978-1-0980-4429-9 (digital)

Christian Faith Publishing, Inc.
832 Park Avenue
Meadville, PA 16335
www.christianfaithpublishing.com

Printed in the United States of America

DEDICATION

I dedicate this book to my grandchildren, present and future, who were the inspiration for writing this book. Grace, Landon, Evelyn, and Elliott

PREFACE

"Ask her doctor about Lupus." Those were the words my father-in-law told my husband, Mike, during a phone call. My father-in-law was a well-respected doctor for over forty-five years in a small town in Missouri, and my husband had been describing my symptoms to him. After three months of futile visits to a dermatologist for a rash, I was getting progressively worse. He had done a couple of skin biopsies, which the results came back as inconclusive and was giving me free samples of skin cream to use which did absolutely nothing for me.

I was also six months pregnant, and the only answer the dermatologist had for me was that I was allergic to my pregnancy! That's right. Allergic to my baby! I thought to myself, *Is he crazy, or am I? If this is indeed some kind of weird reaction to pregnancy, I still have three months to go, I'll never make it!*

After making an appointment with my obstetrician, upon our arrival, my husband had to sign my name as I was unable to hold a pen to write. I had no use of one arm and very little use of the other as my joints had become very painful as well. I had become very good at rolling myself out of bed in the mornings, and my skin would itch intensely when exposed to the outdoor heat. While sitting in my obstetrician's office, I felt as though he took one look at me and knew something was terribly wrong and almost immediately was on his phone making sure I was seen by an internal medicine specialist, ASAP. The rest of the day was spent being examined and talking about how my pregnancy would affect the treatment plan. One of the first things I remember the doctor saying to me was that my right arm was the equivalent of someone with third degree burns, and to complicate matters more, I still needed to be a functioning mom to my two precious boys who were five and two. Thankfully, Mike and I were members of a wonderful, caring church, but it was difficult to go out in public. My sons still needed to get to preschool, but their preschool was at the church we attended, so I knew most everyone would be helpful and understanding of my strange looking face, but the grocery store was a whole different experience.

I was closely monitored for the last trimester. I remember thinking how I can have this disease and it not affect my baby, but I tried not to dwell on such things, but that was a recurring thought. On November 6, 1989, I gave birth to a healthy girl which we named Kimberly Mary Swift. Mary was the name of both of her grandmothers. Then came the issue of breastfeeding. My doctor was anxious to start me on medications, but we could not as long as I was breastfeeding—which I wanted to do—so we compromised that I would, but I agreed I would do so for only a few months so my treatment could begin. The nurse brought Kimberly to my room in her bassinet, and I remember looking over her and thinking, *How am I ever going to do this?* I barely had strength to care for myself, so how was I going to care for this beautiful tiny infant. My daughter needed me, so I prayed that God would give me strength and heal me so I could be the mom my daughter needed me to be.

CHAPTER I

It was a bright, sunny spring morning as I stood outside our home and watched our oldest son, Bradley, walk to his friend's house at the corner of our cul-de-sac to play. I remember my right arm was itching. *Maybe, I got some mosquitoes bites*, I thought, as we had been camping the weekend before. A few days later, the left arm began to itch. *Mosquitoes' bites don't spread*, I thought.

Slowly, the itching was becoming so unbearable I often used a hairbrush to scratch, and I was also developing an unusual rash on my face which strangely resembled the wings of a butterfly over my nose and cheeks. We later learned that a rash on the face that resembles a butterfly is a common characteristic of Lupus. One afternoon, a friend, who used to be my roommate, and I decided to meet at her home for lunch. Becky and I had been very close, sharing a love of country and bluegrass music, and both of us worked in the dental field. I worked for a dentist, and she for an oral surgeon, and at one time, our offices were next to each other. But after we both married, in the ensuing years, life had gotten in the way of us seeing each other regularly, so this lunch date definitely brightened my day. She was shocked to see my rash, so I lifted my shirt for her to see my back, and she quickly exclaimed, "Wow, there is not even room to put a pin head here," referring to the total coverage on my back of the rash.

After receiving the confirmation of lupus, Mike bought every book he could find about lupus as we had never heard of this disease. This was also before the convenience of Google. We wanted and needed to know everything about this unwelcomed intruder to our lives. Is there a cure? Is it, um, you know, fatal? I remember feeling very bad for Mike as we were only five years into our marriage, and he now had a wife with an incurable disease. The wedding vow, "in sickness and in health," was being put to the test rather soon as we were both young and healthy, so this was a shocking revelation to us. It turned our happy world upside down. To make matters worse, Mike's company had merged with another company, and he was let go as a result of the merger, and I will never forget the evening he came home and told me he was unemployed. So here we were with two young children, another on the way, one of us very ill, and no employment. All marriages go through highs and lows, and this was definitely a low, stressful time for us. There is an expression that says, "When God closes one door, he opens another," and fortunately, Mike found another job fairly quickly. In fact, we were doubly blessed as he was offered two jobs at once!

Through our research, we learned that lupus is a complex disease, and it is one of many autoimmune diseases. In people with lupus, something goes wrong with the immune system, as the immune system will attack a person's healthy tissues and organs causing inflammation, swelling, joint pain, a rash, and fatigue. A doctor explained it to me as the body is confused and attacks itself. It also mimics other illnesses, so it can be difficult to diagnose. There is a probability of about 25 percent of women who will experience hair loss which was another of my symptoms. I would wake up in the mornings and find clumps of hair on my pillow. After a referral from my doctor, I made visits to a dermatologist for several months to receive six to eight injections each visit in my scalp for the hair loss. I don't know what was in those shots; I just know it did help to regrow some of my lost hair.

There are two types of lupus. Discoid lupus erythematosus is generally a benign disorder which affects only the skin while systemic lupus erythematosus (also known as SLE) affects not only the skin but many vital organs as well. The cause of lupus is unknown, and roughly 89 percent of lupus patients are women. The highest number of cases is from the teen years to the forties, with the average age being twenty-nine or thirty. Since younger women are most affected, it was maybe why my doctor said to me that she would be much more concerned if I were younger. I was thirty-five when given my diagnosis of systemic lupus erythematosus.

One recurring theme we found while researching lupus was the importance of protection from sun exposure. I first thought that would be difficult for me as we owned a boat at the time and enjoyed camping and boating with our young family and friends. I remember having a mental picture of me skiing while holding an umbrella to protect me from the sun. While, of course, I could never do that, I think that was part of my mindset that I would not let this disease change how I like to live. Instead, I just started buying the highest SPF sunscreens I could find and buying hats! Years later, my obstetrician told me that in all his many years of practice, he had never encountered a patient who developed lupus during her pregnancy. He then asked my permission to use my case in a presentation he would be making at a conference.

My first of many bouts of pneumonia happened when my son, Bradley, was in kindergarten. I volunteered as his class book reader. He returned home from school one day with a large manila envelope and said his teacher had told him to be sure that he gave it to me, and inside were pictures the children had drawn and had written get-well-soon cards. Their pictures were of many random things kindergartens draw like rainbows, flowers, hearts, and stick people. I was so touched. It was many weeks before I was able to return, but I often thought how that large envelope filled with get well wishes from precious children had brightened my day and made me feel a little better.

When my daughter was one, I had the flu which quickly turned into another pneumonia. Walking from one room to the next left me completely exhausted. I struggled to breath, my joints hurt, so basically, I was a mess, physically. Even eating took more energy than I could muster, so cooking was definitely out of the question. Thank goodness, my husband is a good cook and enjoys doing it. My doctor wanted to admit me to the hospital.

"I can't." I said. "I have a lot of kids coming to my house tomorrow for my son's birthday." I don't think my response surprised her because she knew I was going to do everything I could to not let this disease keep me from living my life. My husband would often tell me that I was in denial that I was even sick. I was stubborn and maybe a little foolish as well. She agreed to not admit me as long as I agreed to complete bed rest for several weeks, and I was not to leave my house which I don't think I could have anyway. The birthday party went on as planned as Mike took over and orchestrated the whole event. I had no doubt he could do it as he was a wonderful, involved father, coaching our children's T-ball and soccer teams, Sunday school teacher, and scout leader. Birthday parties were my area of expertise, but I had to let go and concentrate on me and my failing health. Pneumonia was something I dealt with a lot for several years. I started telling my friends that I never get a cold, I just go straight to pneumonia.

During those early years when the lupus was robbing me of my strength and the ability to do even the simplest of tasks, my husband hired a young girl whose name was Tammy, who was his secretary's daughter, to come in once a week and do light housekeeping for me and to help care for the children. She was like an answered prayer to me. My family lives in Florida, and my husband's parents were in Missouri, so we were pretty much on our own with the exception of our church family. When my mother and mother-in-law came to help, I cried when it came time for them to leave. On a Friday afternoon, before Kimberly was born, I received a call from a friend named Faye from our church. Faye and I belonged to the same women's circle, and she was calling to tell me she was on her way to pick up my sons and would be keeping them until the next day so my husband and I could have a break, and she wasn't going to let me say no. She had two sons herself so I knew my boys would have fun. That was an act of kindness I will never forget.

I eventually started responding well to therapy which was a drug called prednisone which is a steroid hormone and hydroxychloroquine also known as Plaquenil which is an antimalarial drug that is used as a suppressant for lupus erythematosus. One of the side effects of Plaquenil is color blindness, so I would routinely have my eyes check. One day, while picking my children up from preschool, I was talking to a friend about my condition and medications. She was aware of the color blindness side effect of Plaquenil, and as we were saying our goodbyes, I slyly told her I liked her red sweater, and I will never forget the look on her face because her sweater was actually brown! After she realized I was joking, we both shared a good laugh. It felt good. One day, I called my husband, excited to tell him that I could close my hand and make a fist. Imagine for a moment being excited at being able to make a fist, but I was, and it was at that moment I really began to believe and see that my prayers were being answered.

There were some very scary episodes along the way. In this book, I will recall those scary episodes; some of which, my children may remember but most they will not. One of those events happened on a routine visit to my lupus doctor (as I affectionately referred to her). After my examination and chest X-ray, she summoned me to her office and proceeded to tell me that I needed to go to an emergency room, ASAP.

"I can't," I said. "I have to pick my children up from school."

"Is there anyone else who can pick your children up?" she replied. Her urgency was becoming alarming to me, but she then went on to explain that I had excess fluid around my lung. I then explained to her that I had played eighteen holes of golf just the day before with my family and had felt fine, and I felt fine now. She relented and told me to go to a pulmonary doctor as soon as I possibly could. Sitting in yet another doctor's office, I was awaiting a procedure called a thoracentesis that would drain the fluid from my lung. During the procedure, I remember the doctor telling me that close to a liter of fluid was coming from my lung. Why I had no symptoms of this remains a mystery to me to this day. The drainage procedure was a success except the fluid kept returning, and after another drainage procedure and the fluid returning, a decision was made to surgically drain the next time the fluid appears. The most I remember about the experience was spending several days in the hospital and being in a lot of pain.

My son, Brian's, third-grade teacher came by to visit and left me a very sweet note because I was asleep from the strong pain medications I had to have. I so hated I missed the chance to visit with her because she was such a special teacher to us, and we all loved her. We later learned that my condition was called exudative plural effusions which is often cause by pneumonia. Autoimmune conditions such as rheumatoid arthritis or lupus can manifest as a plural effusion. After that surgery, I had quite a few years being free of lupus, as my treatment plan was keeping it under control, and during those years, my family experienced some wonderful vacations to the Florida Keys where all of us had the experience of parasailing San Francisco and Boston. It is where we followed the trip of Paul Revere on his famous ride and stood at the bay where the Boston tea party took place, and my son, Brian, and his dad went to the Baseball Hall of Fame in Connecticut where we all had our first experience snow skiing. My children and I even enjoyed a cruise to the Caribbean with my sister and her son. I was able to be involved in my children's school activities, serving on PTA boards, being a room mom, and basically being involved in their lives in and out of school. Life was good. I was very blessed.

During the fall of one year, I was experiencing pain from a dislocated shoulder due to inflammation, and while my husband and I tried our best to never miss any of our children's soccer games, this particular night, my son's soccer game was on a very cold evening. A very nice woman sitting next to me was offering her poncho to wear as she obliviously noticed that I was shivering. I politely declined saying I was fine, but she kept insisting I use her poncho. I whispered to my husband that he was going to have to put this nice lady's poncho on me as there was no way I could lift my arm to do so because just the slightest touch was very painful, so he put it over my head and then off of me with the utmost of care. Good job, dear!

I was still not done with plural effusions though. One evening, I was playing with our dogs, chasing them around our den when I noticed I had become very winded, and walking upstairs left me needing to sit on the top stair as I was completely out of breath. When I mentioned to Mike that chasing our dogs had made me tired, he responded by telling me, "Well, you're not as young as you used to be."

I gave him a look that conveyed my feeling of I can't believe you just said that. I replied, "While that is true, I really don't think that is the problem. I think there's something else going on."

Within the next few days, I made an appointment with another doctor as my original lupus doctor had since retired. After reviewing my X-ray, I was once again told to go to an emergency room. I called Mike and told him the news, but since I knew what they were going to do, he did not need to meet me there. Big mistake. I thought I was being the nice wife because he had a bridge game that night, and I figured that I would be home soon. After arriving at the emergency room, I was led to a treatment room, and the nurse was making the preparations for the drainage procedure.

Suddenly—and I really can't explain why—I was beginning to feel anxious and wanted Mike there with me. *Besides*, I thought, *how would it look to the kids if their mother was in the emergency room and their dad was playing bridge*. Very bad optics! I spotted a phone on a wall across the hall, and I knew they would be starting soon, so I jumped off the table, went to the phone, and called Mike and asked him to come quickly. He didn't make it in time for the procedure. The doctor told me I would be doing some coughing near the end of the drainage, and the coughing began just as he said it would, but it continued until I wasn't able to catch a breath. I was coughing so violently, and being unable to breath, my arms began flailing wildly, and I struggled to say, "I can't breathe." I knocked the instruments off the table onto the floor as I was in full panic mode! Mike arrived after my performance but was there as they moved me to another room for an X-ray which revealed that my lung had collapsed, and after a couple of failed attempts to inflate my lung, it was decided that I needed to be admitted for oxygen and observation. I was discharged two days later.

In 1999, we had an exchange student from Brazil come live with us. He was only to stay for a semester of school but asked if he could stay and finish the school year to better improve his English, and we agreed. After doing the necessary paperwork and attending our orientation meetings with other "parents," the day had finally come to go to the airport and meet our temporarily adopted son. The excitement was building as his plane landed, and Mike and I, along with our kids, waited to see Felipe and welcome him into our lives. He was a handsome young man, eighteen years old, and had a contagious smile. He was also a generous young man as he arrived bearing gifts for everyone which made my kids very happy. After arriving home and opening our gifts it was just a short time before he and our oldest son were kicking around a soccer ball in our driveway, and then, all of them playing video games. The transition was going very well.

We were told at our meetings that we were to incorporate the student into our family life in every way, such as giving him chores to do. He was not a guest. Since his family lived in an apartment in Brazil, he had never had the experience of mowing a lawn, so we made sure he had that opportunity. He actually seemed to enjoy doing some things he had never done before. His spoke English fairly well, so there wasn't a language barrier though he may have had a hard time understanding our daughter as she had the unusual ability to talk like an auctioneer and sounded somewhat British. He played soccer as did all three of our children, so he was a perfect fit for our family. In fact, he was one of the best players on the high school team, and with four kids playing soccer at one time, our lives were a whirlwind of activity. We were constantly on the go, but I actually miss those years. One of my favorite Christmas presents that year was a white sweatshirt from my kids that read "Soccer Mom" in big black letters that I will never part with. That sweatshirt is a reminder of the years that passed too quickly.

I was fortunate not to have any flare ups the year Felipe was with us, and during his time with us, we took him to the arch in St. Louis and Disney World, and he visited both our families in Missouri and Florida. My oldest son went to visit Felipe and his family in Brazil, and he has been back to visit us. This experience was wonderful, and I would recommend to everyone, if you are able, to host an exchange student in your home. One evening, we invited two of his fellow exchange students to our home for dinner except I didn't cook; they did! I turned my kitchen over to them, and they each prepared their favorite meal from their homeland. I suspected they may have called their mothers before this night as they seemed very comfortable and confident making their meals. One student was from Poland, and the other was from Italy, and it was the most varied meal our family had ever eaten. Felipe had become so much a part of our family that I had tears in my eyes at the airport as we said our goodbyes as his year with us had ended. Thanks to technology we have been able to remain in touch.

In 2002, I was needing another surgery for fluid, only this time, they would be doing a procedure called pleurodesis that would put a powder in the lung that would prevent this from happening again. This time, the pain afterward was minimal compared to my first surgery years earlier. I was discharged after a few days and sent home, but on my second day home recovering, it became very difficult for me to breath. My heart was racing, feeling as though it wanted to beat itself out of my chest. I tried everything I could think of to slow down my heart such as lying down, sitting up, walking, deep breaths, shallow breaths—nothing was working. When my husband, Mike, arrived home from work, he immediately recognized the difficulty I was having breathing and insisted we call my doctor.

After the doctor talked to me, he asked to speak with my husband. Mike said the doctor wanted us to meet him at the emergency room. (He later shared that the doctor had told him for us to get to the emergency room as quickly as possible.) At the emergency room, they immediately took me to a room and put me on oxygen, and I quickly began to feel better. *Wonderful,* I thought. Now, I can go back home, except the doctor had other ideas. I was going nowhere except to a room in the hospital as he wanted to keep me on oxygen overnight. Fortunately, my mom and sister were there to help shuttle the kids to and from school. The explanation for my difficulty breathing and racing heart was an allergic reaction to the powder inserted in my lungs.

CHAPTER 2

During my next long stretch of the lupus being in remission, I was able to accompany our church youth group on a mission trip to the poor rural east Tennessee region, doing home repair work and fellow-shipping with the residents. Mike and the children had been several times and were always excited upon returning, talking about what a great time they had. I looked forward to that week as much as they did but for very selfish reasons.

I became queen of my own universe for that week, with no meals to prepare, no laundry to do, no taxing kids here and there; just a week to myself to do as I pleased. I was in my own paradise, but after a few years, I was beginning to feel left out, so I shocked my family by declaring that I wanted to go. "Sign me up!" I said.

Surprised and confused, my children and husband said things like, "Are you sure you want to do this." I heard remarks like, "You won't last the week," and "You'll hurt yourself."

With responses like those, I don't think my family had much faith in me, but I like to think they were proud of their mother for taking this huge step. I just felt I needed to go and see what they loved about this trip. Halfway through my week, I still had not found it. It was hard work. It was long days of labor in the hot sun, and knowing I needed to be very careful about my sun exposure, I took every precaution. I was lucky to be placed in the same cabin as my daughter, and as much as I wanted to go to her bunk and hang out with her, I knew I needed to give her space. She was very good at giving me my space as well! At the end of the week, I don't believe many people knew we were mother and daughter.

One of our jobs was to build new steps to a home of two elderly men who were brothers. Upon arriving on the property, some of the youth couldn't believe that someone actually lived in the home as it was quite dilapidated. Nearing the end of building their steps, the power company came and turned off the power to their home. That made everyone very sad, and it also made it very difficult to finish as our saws needed electricity, but because of a generous neighbor, who loaned us a long extension cord, we were able to finish their steps using the electricity from his home. The men then joined us in a prayer circle before we left, and one of the brothers prayed a very moving, powerful prayer that made one of the youths wonder if he was a minister. The actions of the neighbor reminded me of the Bible passage, "We are our brother's keeper."

By the end of the week, I had begun to see what my family loved about this experience because the feeling you get when you do for others is incredible, and the fellowship with the people you meet during the week is inspiring, and they are so appreciative of you. The evening worship services were very moving as the teenagers spoke of the way they saw Christ at work in their lives and in the lives of the people they were serving. I was personally moved by seeing this group of teenagers giving up a week of their summer vacation to come be the hands and feet of God, and I thought the future of our country was in very good hands.

One of the evening worship services included a foot washing ceremony. The camp staff washed the feet of the adult leaders and prays with them, then, the leaders washed the feet of the youth and prayed over them. As I made my way around the circle, I noticed a girl quietly crying. As I got closer to her, I was asking God to give me the words she needed to hear, and then, I realized she was a girl I had been critical of earlier in the day. God made me realize I was not in a position to judge, and it was very humbling how God used me to reach out to her after I had been critical of her. My experience with this mission trip and others that followed made me love two verses from James 2:14, 17, "What good is it, my brothers and sisters, if you say you have faith but do not have works? So faith by itself, if it has no works, is dead."

Things were going really well until round three of pneumonia hit. I was home alone one morning, preparing to take a shower, when

I suddenly began to shake uncontrollably. *What in the world is happening?* I thought. I proceeded to get in the shower, and sitting on the floor, I let the water run over me as hot as I could without scalding myself. It wasn't helping as the shaking was continuing. I was beginning to think maybe I should call 911 because I was becoming very scared that something terrible was happening to me. Instead, I got into bed in my winter robe and covered myself with blankets. Gradually, the shaking was subsiding. A doctor's appointment reveled pneumonia—again. After a round of antibiotics and rest, I was like new again.

I was experiencing many years in remission which I regularly prayed for, and I had taken a job at a nearby church preschool. I had subbed a lot at various preschools when the children were younger, but my children were now high-school age, so this was my first five-day-a-week employment in many years. We were fortunate that my husband had been successful in his career as a certified public accountant, and we both wanted me to be a stay-at-home mom. My younger son expressed displeasure at my going to work, but I explained to him that high schools don't have room mothers or class parties like the elementary age does, and I will still be serving a board position on the PTA. He replied that he just liked knowing I was home. That warmed my heart. The preschool just happened to be next to the high school, and much to my disbelief and surprise, the school would let me leave once a month to attend the PTA meetings without docking my pay. I always felt it was because the director understood the importance of parental involvement in education.

On a cold winter morning, I was running late for work at the preschool and was feeling stressed about arriving late. I've never been a big fan of cold weather, and it may have something to do with being raised in a warm-weather state. I like cold weather only if it's snowing! As I arrived into my classroom, I noticed that my fingertips were very white and tingling. I showed them to my co-teacher, and she told me it was Raynaud's syndrome, and she suggested I hold my hands under warm water until the feeling and color return.

After I returned home from the school day, I immediately went to my computer and Googled "Raynaud's." What I learned is that the symptoms of Raynaud's are most commonly associated with cold and stress. Well, imagine what I thought! It's no wonder my fingertips were white and tingling that morning as I was experiencing both! Upon further reading, I also learned that it is caused by an overreaction of blood vessels in the extremities to temperature and stress. In normal physiology, when a person's body is exposed to cold, the blood vessels in the extremities become narrowed and slow down blood supply to the fingers and toes. This is to prevent heat loss from these areas and preserve the body's core temperature. Similarly, in times of stress, the fight-or-flight response begins, and blood flow to the fingers and toes is reduced as the body tries to conserve blood to the vital organs and muscles. With Raynaud's, these responses are exaggerated, causing the symptoms. The extremities can look pale or even blue and cold as no warm blood is reaching those areas.

There are two types of Raynaud's. Primary Raynaud's appear independently, and its cause is unknown. The other is secondary Raynaud's which is caused by an underlying condition. One of the conditions that can cause Raynaud's is—you guessed it—lupus. In fact, the National Resource Center on Lupus reports that one third of people with lupus will have Raynaud's. It appears that the older I become, the Raynaud's has become more frequent. There have been times when I've been in the grocery store, and my fingers have become white; a rather scary sight indeed! On a few occasions, I have worn gloves in the grocery store. My daughter sometimes experiences Raynaud's in her feet, but she doesn't have lupus, so hers would be primary Raynaud's.

CHAPTER 3

I have been off medications for lupus for many years now, and in the summer of 2007, my son, Brian, was asked to be an adult leader on a youth mission trip, and I was very excited because I was also going as an adult volunteer. I had the experience of being on a mission trip with my daughter and, now, with my son, and I was thrilled.

A few days before our departure, I developed a nagging, lingering cough. Thinking about the trip, I decided to see a doctor before leaving, and to no surprise, I was told I had pneumonia, and we were scheduled to leave the very next day! *Not again, not now!* I thought! Upon returning home, my son and his fiancée were there, and as soon as I walked in the door, he asked me, "What did the doctor say?"

Tears started streaming down my face as I could barely speak and tell him it was pneumonia. He came to me and gave me a hug and said he was sorry this had happened again. He was shocked when I said I was still going.

"You can't," he replied. "You have pneumonia!"

"I'll have my medications with me, I'll be fine," I insisted.

Besides, I reasoned with myself that I would take many breaks and not overexert myself. I'm sure Mike and Brian thought I was being stubborn and in denial again. The first day was just traveling. We were three days into our week when things started to unravel for me. The second day at our worksite, my energy was completely depleted. We were putting a new roof on a lady's porch, and my job was to move the aluminum slabs from one pile to another, closer to the house. Not a hard job, but it did involve a lot of walking back-and-forth, and after a while, I was beginning to feel like I was about to collapse. I was feeling so exhausted. I went and laid down in the backseat of the other leader's SUV. I was crying. The heat and pneumonia had drained me of my strength and stamina. After a few minutes, I composed myself and went back to join the group which, again, were high school students from various parts of the country.

I had kept my illness secret from my group; only the other adult leaders knew of my illness. Lying in my bed that night, thinking of what had happened earlier, I began to wonder if I had made a mistake coming. *Maybe, I wasn't getting better*, I thought. I would return to the cabin before anyone else to take my meds, and I also worried if my coughing was keeping anyone awake. It was as if God decided it was time for me to be free of this illness because, the next day, I truly felt as thou I had turned a corner and began feeling better each remaining day.

Near the end of the week, I was feeling so well that I began to sing karaoke in the van along with the kids, even using a hairbrush as a microphone. We were having such a wonderful time, and those kids probably wondered what I had been drinking as I had been rather subdued for most of the week, conserving my energy. I, then, shared with them that I had been sick with pneumonia for most of the week; needless to say, they were impressed and started calling me Wonder Woman. Embarrassing as that was, they were an awesome group of kids, and on our last day together, we were allowed time to go into town and do some shopping and buy inexpensive gifts for one another. The other leader knew of a quiet, beautiful place with a large cross where we went to share our gifts with one another, and one of the gifts from "my kids" was a toy microphone! On our last night, we had a communion service, and I was served communion by my son, and that was a very special moment for me.

Not all of our jobs involved building as, one time, we painted a lady's patio furniture after which she asked if we would come inside and help her and her mother shell a bushel of peas, and while we were all busy shelling peas, the elderly mother shared her faith journey with us. Another time, we cleared overgrown brush and pulled weeds from a woman's flower garden, and while we were hard at work, she was inside, making us an apple pie after which we enjoyed around her kitchen table complete with ice cream!

A few weeks after returning home, I received a letter from a girl in my group who had come from Kansas with her church. She wrote about how much that week meant to her and that she really loved having me as her leader. That letter meant a lot to me because it reassured me that, maybe, I was making a difference, even if in a small way. I was very blessed to be able to accompany our youth group on several mission trips and also very blessed that my children didn't mind having their mom on "their" trips. Other missions outreach took us to Cincinnati where we worked each day at a day care center in urban Cincinnati, an Indian reservation in Oklahoma and Minneapolis where my son, Brian, taught English to the Somalia children, just to name a few. Within the next few years, Brian married, and we welcomed a wonderful lady named Katie to our family.

CHAPTER 4

In the fall of 2008, we had taken a trip to visit our longtime friends, Mike and Mari Pautler, in San Francisco. My husband and Mike became friends in college, both majored in accounting and continued their friendship after graduation. We married the same year—only a month apart—and even took some trips together when our children were young. Mike's career moved him around the country quite a bit, and our children used to say that some of our best vacations were to wherever the Pautlers were living.

On this trip, it was just by the grace of God that I lived through it. On our first night there, we had taken some wine glasses and a bottle of wine down by the water. They have a beautiful home overlooking the San Francisco bay. Suddenly, I started feeling nauseous, and I began to look around for a place I could go and vomit if it came to that. Never mentioning that I was feeling bad, we headed back to the house for a lovely dinner that Mari had prepared, but I, instead, headed to our restroom where I spent the rest of the evening and most of the night violently ill with severe, continual cramping, vomiting, and diarrhea.

My throat felt like it was burning, and I remember banging on the wall, pleading to God to please make this stop. "Please, take away this pain," I cried. Fortunately, I had my cell phone with me and called my husband and asked him to come, and upon him opening the door, I said to him, "We may need to go the hospital." I had had a history of bad stomach issues in the past, but nothing like this. Ever.

"Are you sure?" he replied.

"Let's wait a little longer and see if it subsides," I said.

As crazy as this sounds, one of the reasons I wanted to avoid going to the hospital if I could was that I was afraid I would throw up in our friends' car. Looking back, I realize what a dumb reason that was! I never made it to dinner that night. Instead, I spent most of my night trying to sleep on the bathroom floor with a heating pad on my stomach, but eventually, I was able to stumble to the spare bedroom and sleep. I awoke the next morning, showered, and joined everyone outside sitting on their patio, and after just a few minutes and refusing breakfast, I said I had to go back to sleep. The first day of my California vacation was being wasted by my inability to stay awake after a traumatic night. The next day, the guys were going to play golf while Mari took me around San Francisco to see the sights. Feeling very weak and drained, I had mentioned that I didn't feel as though I could do a lot of walking.

One of the things I had said I wanted to experience was a ride on the cable cars, but I was struggling to keep up and was also experiencing a great thirst, but after stopping for a rest and a drink, we proceeded to the cable car station. After seeing the long line for tickets, I told Mari that I could not stand in that long line as my legs felt as though they could not hold me up any longer, so she purchased the tickets, and my wish of riding a cable car had been fulfilled. We were all unaware of the severity of my condition. I thought I had gotten some food poisoning from the restaurant we had stopped at for lunch on the way home from the airport. I was wrong.

After a few days, they drove us to Camarillo where we would be staying with my husband's brother for a few days, and along the way, we stopped for lunch in San Luis Obispo, but I was only able to take a few bites as my stomach felt full even though I had eaten very little since that awful night. On our last night there, I began to run a fever. There were plans to go out for dinner that evening, but I opted out because of the fever and stayed behind, trying to quench my increasing thirst, even calling Mike to stop at a grocery store for a box of banana popsicles. I didn't sleep much that night, waking up numerous times for something to drink.

While sitting in the LA airport, my husband was on the phone with my doctor back in Memphis, trying to make me an appointment for that afternoon. I still had eaten very little during the week, and being a doctor's son, he probably knew the fever indicated an infection in my body. I also found it difficult to find a comfortable position to sit, so that four-hour flight was a challenge. Midway through the flight, I began to feel nauseous again, and as I stood to head to the restrooms in the rear of the plane, I noticed a lot of people standing in the aisle. *I hope they're just stretching*, I thought, *because I needed the restroom and fast!* My worst fear came true as, yes, they were all waiting on the restroom. I noticed a flight attendant in the rear galley, and I quickly went to her and asked for a bag because I was going to throw up. She quickly brought me one, and I knelt to my knees and proceeded to make everyone move further from me. She, then, also made sure I got into the restroom next!

Upon returning to my seat, I calmly told Mike that I had just thrown up, and without taking his eyes off the book he was reading, he replied, "Oh, that's too bad."

Upon our arrival at the doctor's office, they took an X-ray and drew some blood, then, I was told to go the emergency room as they did not have the equipment to properly diagnose me and that my blood counts were off the charts. So off to another emergency room I go. My first clue that I would be admitted and not going home was when the nurse brought my urine sample into the treatment room and put it on the counter, and I noticed it was a very dark color. Now, I am not a nurse, but I don't think you need to be to know that urine should never be that color; if it is, then, you are sick!

I was immediately sent for an MRI which revealed that my colon had ruptured that dreadful night. My surgeon later told me that had an abscess not formed, which was the size of a large grapefruit, and attached itself to my appendix, I would have died from septic poisoning. He also told us that if we had gone to the hospital the night of the rupture, they would have done emergency surgery, and I would have had to wear a colostomy bag for a while. He, then, added that I had a very high pain threshold which could have turned out to not be a good thing that night. The rupture was healing, but I spent twelve days in the hospital with a tube inserted in my side while the abscess was drained, and I had a strong sense of deja vu as I remembered being in a similar situation being in a hospital with tubes inserted in my side, draining fluids from my lungs.

I lived on broth and pudding. My doctor told me that I was too ill and too weak to operate now and that I was to go home and gain some weight, and then, they would remove part of my colon in a few months. Mike joked that he wished a doctor would tell him to go home and gain some weight! During my stay, I was totally caught off guard and surprised when my oldest son, Bradley, walked into my room. He lived outside of Nashville and came to see me as a complete surprise, and needless to say, I was crying happy tears.

The reason for the rupture happening was that I had a section of my colon that had some diverticulum which are abnormal pouches or sacs that protrude from the colon. Sometimes, these openings can become clogged and inflamed and, in my case, burst. I had been told I had some diverticula by a doctor just a few months prior after a colonoscopy but was also told that they rarely cause a problem. Well, I guess I was an exception to that belief.

During my hospital stay, I was treated by what seemed like a team of doctors. I remember the pathologist came into my room, stood at the foot of my bed, and listed numerous difficult-to-pronounce words I had never heard before. He was telling me the names of all the bacteria they found in the abscess fluid, and the only one I recognized was E. coli. Another doctor recommended that I have a blood transfusion, but I don't remember why. After discussing this with Mike, we declined the transfusion. My surgeon was wonderful in that he explained things in such a thorough way that we knew exactly what had happened and why. He drew on a whiteboard a diagram of my colon, pointed where the diverticula were, and what the surgery would do.

I was discharged and sent home with an arsenal of pills. Six to eight a day I was to take, and some were large pills. Now, I have never liked taking pills especially large ones as they tend to make me choke and gag. So I spent my days taking pills, choking and gagging, taking pills, and chocking and gagging. I was so miserable I wanted to inquire about having an IV pole at home to administer the antibiotics intravenously but never did. Since the doctor's orders were to gain weight, on the way home, we stopped at a Sonic, and I feasted on a double cheeseburger, fries, and milkshake—my first meal in weeks, and it tasted so delicious. My weight had dropped to nearly 100 pounds, so I figured I would be having more meals like that one.

I was discharged on Halloween and still very weak, so my husband had to greet all the princesses, ghosts, and superheroes that visited us that night. He has never liked Halloween, so that was not a fun evening for him. He would have preferred to just turn off the lights, but I have always enjoyed Halloween and wanted our house to participate.

Three months later, in February of the following year, I had my colon-resection surgery where they took out five feet of a curve in my colon where the diverticula were and, then, reattached the colon. That hospital stay was about ten days, and I remember there were several days that I thought I would be discharged only to be disappointed, to wait another day. When my release finally did happen, I remember on the drive home I started releasing all the emotions of relief and joy I felt to finally have this health scare behind us as it had been a very difficult five months. Happy tears once again! Once home, our Sunday-school class kept us well-fed with meals arriving almost daily. Everyone's act of kindness reminded me how God is a God of goodness and mercy and that he is with us when bad things happen and that he holds us in our most challenging moments.

For several months, I had recurring dreams of Mike trying to wake me up the day after the rupture, and I would not wake up. I was dead. I attributed this to my doctor telling me I was very lucky to be alive. Gradually and thankfully, those dreams faded away.

CHAPTER 5

It has now been several years since that event, and I have enjoyed and treasured every moment of my life. In January of 2011, we had a significant snowfall. We would normally get one or two snowfalls a year but usually just a dusting, but this one measured several inches.

My neighbor Tina was taking her son and some other neighborhood children to a nearby middle school to sled down a hill at the back of the school and asked if I would like to join them. My inner child is one to never pass on a fun time, so I immediately said yes, and it was a decision I would soon regret for the rest of my life. We walked to the school, and the slope was covered in snow, and we were ready to have some fun. I put my sled down, sat on it, and proceeded to slide quickly down the hill. Unbeknownst to all of us, there was a frozen solid lump of snow at the bottom of the hill, and my sled hit that frozen hump dead center. I quickly went airborne and hit the ground with such a jolt that I was thrown off the sled and landed on my back in the snow.

There was such an intense pain that surged through my body that I was immediately scared, and I remember moving my toes, legs, and fingers just to see if they would move, and they did, and I felt so relieved. Tina slid beside me and asked if I was okay, and I said no but that I would be all right; I just need to lie there a minute. I somehow managed to climb back up the hill but knew my fun day of sledding was over after just one ride down the hill. The pain was so intense I wanted to cry, but I didn't want to upset the children, so I didn't. I just laid in the snow, waiting until everyone was ready to leave, but everyone wanted then to go to a nearby church which also had a nice hill perfect for sledding, so I slowly walked with the group to the church. Knowing that we had walked to these places, I also knew there was no way I would be able to walk home. The pain was just too much. Fortunately, Tina's husband came to watch the fun and took us all home in his pickup truck.

Upon arriving in my house, I immediately found a heating pad and laid on my sofa, thinking I had pulled or strained a muscle. Sleeping that night was very difficult, and the next day was a work day for me, so the next morning, I proceeded to gently raise myself out of bed, and as soon as I put my feet on the floor, the pain was nearly paralyzing. I gingerly walked to a phone and told my boss that I could not come to work because I could barely move, and after telling her what had happened, she joked something about me being a kamikaze pilot which I actually found amusing despite my pain. My job was only two days a week, so fortunately, I had the next day to recover. I was able to go to work, but I was moving very carefully, and my coworker was a very sweet elderly lady who looked a lot like my mom and was very understanding of my discomfort, even offering me a Tylenol as I slouched in one of our rooms' rocking chairs. I was working in a baby room at a preschool, so I really wasn't much help to her that day. It felt good to slouch while sitting as opposed to sitting straight.

My accident happened on a Monday, and by Friday, I was still having so much pain. I made an appointment with my doctor, and after an X-ray revealed nothing broken, I was given muscle relaxants and told to return if my pain continued. I returned after a week with no improvement and was referred for an MRI which revealed I had a stress fracture at the T12 bone in my back.

I was given a back brace to wear for about six weeks along with physical therapy appointments. We were told the fracture would eventually heal on its own, but surgery was also an option. We decided to wait it out since I was still able to function somewhat normally with a few restrictions such as not lifting anything over five pounds, and for that reason, I was moved to another classroom with older children. There were triggers I knew to be wary of such as sitting or standing for long periods of time, but essentially, I just carried on. After waiting for a little over a year for the fracture to heal, I decided to have the operation, but there was something I needed to do first.

CHAPTER 6

My husband and I have been involved in a group called Emmaus for many years which is a retreat for people to deepen their walk with Christ. One year, I was asked to be a group leader and give a talk to the group of women on a retreat. My husband and two of my children had done this many times, but this would be my first. The retreat consisted of several daily talks—some by clergy and some by the leaders of the retreat—skits planned and performed by the participants, and of course, a lot of good food prepared and served by previous retreat attendees. My sister would also be on this particular retreat, so that made it extra special. I didn't have a lot of experience speaking before groups with the exception of my PTA days and being a Sunday-school officer, so I was somewhat nervous about giving this talk.

My topic would be "Christian Action" which encourages people to put their faith into action, and in turn, you have become a blessing to someone. I ended my talk by telling the women a story about a church in Strasburg, Germany, that was totally destroyed during World War II, but a statue of Christ survived with only its hands blown off, and at the foot of this statue was a plaque that read, "Christ has no hands but ours." After working on the talk for weeks, it was time to start rehearsing in front of my husband and daughter, and even my dog had to listen to me.

My husband, daughter, son, and brother, who had come to surprise my sister, and some dear friends prayed with me, moments before my talk was to begin, and as I made my way to the conference room and stood outside the door, I felt a calm come over me, and I felt very confident as I walked to the podium to deliver God's message to these women. When I explained this to a dear friend, she told me it was the Holy Spirit working to take away my fears. The weekend was a success with several women dedicating their lives to having a closer relationship to Jesus and being the hands and feet of Jesus. Just a few days after the retreat ended, I had the surgery to repair my back. I can't say I was one hundred percent pain free, but there was some improvement.

Unbelievably, I experienced another stress fracture just below the first one a few years later, not from an accident but from a very bad case of bronchitis. The doctors said, most likely, every time I coughed, the spine would hit the cement in the T12 bone which repaired the first fracture. I had heard of people breaking ribs from coughing but never this. So now, I just always have a pillow with me if I'm taking a long trip to place behind my back.

In July of 2013, my church was taking their annual mission trip to Kenya. My daughter had gone a few years earlier, and I had always thought about going. In church one morning, we saw in the church bulletin the deadline was fast approaching, and my husband—knowing of my desire to go—whispered to me if I wanted to go, I had better decide quickly. I was somewhat shocked and surprised he would say that to me because he never seemed supportive of me doing this because of my health history. I kept hearing voices (yes, you read that right), telling me to do this and another telling me not to. In the end, I felt there were three deciding factors that would put me in Africa. The first was surviving the colon rupture. Obviously, it was not my time, and maybe, I survived because God wants me to do this. Second was a six-week Sunday-school class video lesson based on a book titled *If You Want to Walk on Water, You've Got to Get Out of the Boat* by John Ortberg. That lesson left me so inspired, and I thought about it long after it ended.

The video series challenged us to stop sailing through life in our vessels surrounded by only our friends, family, jobs, and possessions and get out of our comfort zones once in a while, face our fears, and discover what God has planned for us. The last was a favorite hymn titled "Here I Am, Lord." I feel the chorus of the hymn speaks directly to me. The words are: "Here I am, Lord. It is I, Lord. I have heard you calling in the night. I will go, Lord, if you lead me. I will hold your people in my heart." So I took a deep breath and made the call asking to go to Africa.

And after the longest plane ride of my life, we landed in Nairobi, Kenya, where we spent the night and the next morning loaded on a bus for a long ride to Maua. The group met for several weeks before our departure to get to know one another, and several of the team members were seasoned veterans having been several times before, and I knew them fairly well from church so that was comforting to me. The trip was amazing! My only other trips out of the country had been on luxury cruise liners with the very best accommodations. I must say, though, our hotel was very nice, but we were advised to not drink the water from the tap, and the toilet and shower were in a very tiny room.

We were paired two to a room, and we slept with mosquito nets over our beds. Our main mission was to support a mission hospital in rural Kenya and its outreach to the community, specifically programs for AIDS orphans. We delivered several thousand dollars of medication and medical supplies to the hospital and volunteered at a local clinic, distributing the supplies and assisting the doctors. After morning worship, we would go to one of our several job sites. One of our jobs was building a two-room home for an AIDS orphan family. Getting to the construction site was not easy. We needed to walk down a rocky slope, cross a river on a shaky bridge, and then, climb up a steep, winding trail.

Children would gather at the worksite, and whenever one of us were taking a break, which was highly encouraged, we interacted with them. I found myself teaching the kids how to play London Bridge. The sound of their laughter when one of them had the "bridge" fall on them was like a beautiful symphony. We also provided a vacation-Bible-school type experience for the children from a school with games, songs, and crafts, and one of the children's favorite activities was chasing after bubbles. We also spent time at a Methodist bio-intensive agricultural center with AIDS orphans. They would be getting some valuable agricultural training while we were doing some work around the grounds, some of which I'm sure some of us had never done before. Some of our team members may have been raised on a farm, but I wasn't one of them.

One of our jobs was to paint the inside of pig stalls with the pigs still inside. They're really sweet creatures, but my pig kept licking off the creosote as fast as I could paint it on. And if we were in their way, they weren't at all shy about nudging us aside, though it was hard for us to do the same. At the end of their training, there was a graduation ceremony where the youth received a Certificate of Training diploma of which they were so immensely proud of, as for a lot of these youth, it will most likely be on the only recognition of education they will receive. It was a joyous evening. Our last few days there, we went on a safari tour, and to see God's majestic creatures in their natural habitat was absolutely incredible! We live in a world where we are so abundantly blessed, so to come out of my comfort zone or "bubble" in my upscale suburban America to make this trip to Africa was such an incredible, eye-opening experience. I felt very blessed to be there and was grateful I listened to the voice that said go.

Mosquito nets over our beds

Building the house

"Smile"

The children loved Stickers

"My Pig"

Local Market

Long and winding steep trail to house

Earlier, I quoted James 2:17, which said, "So faith by itself, if it has no works, is dead," and I've shared my mission experiences, but works doesn't have to be a weeklong trip away from your family. It can be as simple as checking on the well-being of an elderly neighbor. Many communities have numerous volunteer opportunities. All it takes is a servant heart and a willing spirit. While sitting in a doctor's office, I read a magazine article which said volunteering can boost your happiness and improve your overall health and could possibly help with some symptoms of depression. So the next time you may be feeling a little down or sad, try volunteering in some way. It may just help to lift your mood and brighten your day.

CHAPTER 7

In the summer of 2014, I began noticing bumps appearing on my legs, so I made an appointment to see a dermatologist. She was unsure what was causing this but suspected it could be related to lupus and gave me the option of a biopsy which I definitely wanted. We had no answers to what this was, and the biopsy should provide one. After the appointment, I flew to Florida to be with my father who was receiving a pacemaker. He was ninety years old and in relatively good health for someone that age, but surgeries are never without risk, and I wanted to be there.

Waiting during his surgery, I received a call from my daughter, telling me to call my dermatologist. She had the results from the biopsy. The diagnosis was polyarteritis nodosa or PAN for short, and after receiving this diagnosis, I began to think of my life as the arcade game, Whack A Mole, where one thing after another would pop up, and doctors and I would need to knock it down. PAN is one of several vasculitis diseases that occurs when there is inflammation throughout the arterial wall and classically affect medium-sized arteries located deep in the deep dermis. Men are twice as likely to be affected than women, and most cases appear in the fourth or fifth decade, although it can occur at any age. Vasculitis can accompany infections or rheumatic diseases such as systemic lupus erythematosus, but in most of the cases, the cause is unknown, though immune system abnormality is a common feature.

When I called my doctor with this diagnosis, he found it hard to believe as he told me it is very rare for a person to have two autoimmune diseases, and he seemed unsure on how to treat this. On one of my appointments, he said he had consulted with his colleagues and even his med-school professor for guidance on what my treatment should be. I asked if I should go to the Mayo Clinic as that would have been easy for me to do as there was one close to my family in Florida or John Hopkins Hospital, but he said no; he thought I could be treated there. The treatment of PAN has improved dramatically in the past couple of decades, but before this improved treatment, PAN was usually fatal within weeks to months, but in most cases of PAN, now, if diagnosed early enough, the disease can be controlled and often cured.

One of the symptoms of PAN is weight loss. My family had been telling me I was getting too thin, but I didn't really see it, as I was eating as I always had, and I have always been a small-framed person much like my mother. Until one day, I stepped out of the shower, and for the first time, I saw what my family had been telling me. I looked like a poster for anorexia. My cheeks looked like canyons as my weight had dropped to ninety-five pounds, and I didn't know why until given this diagnosis. I was also dealing with another symptom—renal artery vasculitis, also known as proteinuria, which leads to protein in the urine which meant there was kidney involvement. My doctor did a kidney biopsy to determine if there was lupus involvement with the kidney, but the biopsy showed no active lupus, just its presence at one time. I was put on a high dose of prednisone and was lowering the dose every two weeks. Anyone who has been on high doses of prednisone knows what difficulties that can bring. It disrupted my sleep. I found myself wide awake at odd hours in the early morning, so I would usually read a book or sometimes scan the TV channels. I did discover there's nothing good to watch on TV at 3:00 a.m. I needed to eat every four hours which helped me to regain my weight, and whenever we would eat out, I wasn't asking for a doggie bag as I would normally do.

In early January of 2017, I started not feeling well, mostly with laryngitis and a steadily climbing fever. After several days with a high fever, I made an appointment with a doctor and was told I had double pneumonia. After my many bouts with pneumonia, I could easily tell the difference with both lungs being involved as the recovery time took much longer, and speaking was very difficult.

We have since moved to the east-Tennessee region to be closer to two of our children and grandchildren, and I hope to live a very long and remaining-healthy life and continuing to do mission work. I only wish my mother could have been with me during some of the later scary and trying times. God has blessed me in so many ways with a husband that is by my side through it all and a family that has made me very proud and I love so dearly. Remember to thank God for each and every day.

> Do all the good you can
> By all the means you can
> In all the ways you can
> In all the places you can
> At all the times you can
> To all the people you can
> As long as you ever can. (John Wesley)

ABOUT THE AUTHOR

Linda Swift lives in Tennessee with her husband and has three grown children and four grandchildren. She enjoys the theatre, traveling, reading, hiking, the beach, and spending time with family. She hopes her experience will offer hope and encouragement for someone with lupus.

CPSIA information can be obtained
at www.ICGtesting.com
Printed in the USA
LVHW041638040623
748851LV00038B/383